Make Your Own
Plush Pals

Victoria Maderna

Dover Publications, Inc.
Mineola, New York

Bibliographical Note

Make Your Own Plush Pals is a new work, first published by
Dover Publications, Inc., in 2010.

Library of Congress Cataloging-in-Publication Data

Maderna, Victoria.
    Make your own plush pals / Victoria Maderna.
       p. cm.
    ISBN-13: 978-0-486-47674-2 (pbk.)
    ISBN-10: 0-486-47674-X (pbk.)
       1. Soft toy making—Juvenile literature. I. Title.

TT174.3.M354 2010
745.592'4—dc22
                                                                2010011384

Manufactured in the United States by Courier Corporation
47674X01
www.doverpublications.com

Table of Contents

Introduction

My goal for this book is to give you guidelines to make a few soft toys and have tons of fun in the process!

The straightforward instructions will allow you to get the same results I did. I've tried my best to be as clear as possible, and to make these creatures varied in type, shape, and complexity so you can find something that suits your taste and expectations.

I also want this book to be a valuable resource for those who want to make their own creations. The instructions can be a stepping-stone, a first approach to create creatures from your imagination. If you follow all the instructions in this book, you will have a strong understanding of the process involved. I've included some tips and ideas at the end of the book to help you.

Basic Crafting Materials

Although many of the items used to make the plush pals can vary from one stuffed creature to the other, there are some basic things that you will always need:

Thread: I use polyester thread for pretty much everything. I use embroidery thread as well, but it's not necessary.

Scissors: To cut, fabric scissors need to be very sharp. It is best to have two pairs of scissors: one to cut fabric and one to cut paper or cardboard.

Straight Pins to piece together fabric for sewing.

Sewing Needles in various sizes.

Chalk/Pencil/Fabric Marker: Any mark-making tool that doesn't bleed. It can be permanent or one that washes away easily.

Glue: I recommend both fabric and paper glue.

Scanner or **Photocopier** is needed to copy the patterns.

Thick Paper/Thin Cardboard: This will make your patterns sturdier, and easier to use. I use cardboard from cereal and cookie boxes.

- -

Fabrics

Trying different fabrics and materials is a lot of fun when making stuffed creatures. I would like to encourage you to give your own spin to the patterns I've included here and divert from my instructions as much as you like. I love going shopping for fabrics. I buy anything that catches my eye or that gives me an interesting idea for a design. It's important to have something in mind when choosing any fabric.

First of all, it's important that the fabric is not too rigid, especially if your design has a lot of curves. Fabrics that are soft and flexible and stretch a bit are the best choice. Make sure they aren't too flexible or the stuffing may become lumpy. One exception to this rule is the Cubefish (*Page 47*). The cube base shape is perfect for rigid fabrics such as denim, corduroy,

or canvas. For this toy, the straighter the sides are and the more defined the seams, the better. It's the perfect shape to make use of fabric that doesn't work with curvy, or rounded shapes.

The second thing I check for when buying fabrics is fraying. I try to get fabrics that don't fray too much, otherwise I would have to leave a generous allowance when cutting. This may make the seams bulge when you turn the creature inside out. When using fabrics for appliqués (*Page 8*) it is crucial to choose a fabric that frays the least amount possible, if at all.

When I'm unsure of how a creature will turn out, or just don't want to risk it, I go back to the fabrics that are, for me, one-hundred-percent reliable: felt and fleece. They're soft, they don't fray, and they are easy to sew. I prefer to use fleece for the main shape and felt for appliqués. You will see this combination used throughout these pages, although I tried to include some variations. Fleece has just the right amount of flexibility and looks great when stuffed. It is definitely my favorite fabric for these projects.

I also love working with plush and fur fabrics, although the rigidity varies a lot from one to the other; you have to go by the way they feel. The hair length has a lot of influence on the final look of the stuffed creature: longhaired fur can be problematic with small shapes, but can be very forgiving with the neatness of the stitches and will cover pretty much every mistake. You will need to take some time to free the hair that gets trapped in the seams in the sewing process. The thickness of longhaired plush can also be troublesome for machine sewing, especially if you have more layers in between (such as limbs or wings). Shorthaired plush behaves more like normal fabric, but is not as forgiving, and doesn't look as good in my opinion, although it may be a better choice for small plush toys.

There are countless other options you can explore such as synthetic leather, vinyl, rubber, and plastic sheets: if it can be sewn (or glued) you are good to go!

Stuffing

There are many things you can use to stuff your soft toys. The ones I've made for this book are all filled with polyester fiberfill: it's very soft and light, washable, and it fills the fabric very uniformly. It comes in regular and hypoallergenic varieties. I thoroughly recommend it.

You can always try out other stuffing materials such as cotton, wool, foam rubber, and polystyrene foam. When I test and make prototypes of my patterns I often use fabric leftovers to fill them out. (I keep all those tiny pieces of fabric that remain after making a plush toy in a bag so I can use them later.) I've also seen soft toys filled with cherry hearts, rice, beans, and even one that was made of clear rubber and filled with little colored plastic toys. Although I like my toys to be lightweight, you can achieve interesting things when they're heavier, especially when posing them. It really depends on the look and feel you want to achieve.

Eyes

There are many types of eyes available for your plush toy: plastic, solid, googly, buttons, fabric—choose what you like best for your creatures!

Each kind of eye has to be attached in a different way: buttons and fabric cut eyes can be sewn or glued (or both), plastic eyes have to be glued, child-safe eyes have a shaft that punches through thin fabric. For thick fabric you might have to make holes in the fabric with a cutter. The eyes are then secured to a plastic piece from inside of the toy, although you may want to glue them as well.

These are, of course, the most standard options. You can also use beads, seeds, pebbles, old coins, felt balls, anything you can think of and can attach somewhat safely is fair game. If you have any other crafting or artistic skills such as felting, embroidering, sculpting, knitting, crocheting, or painting take advantage of them to create eyes and facial features for your plush pals.

Wrong and Right Sides of the Fabric: A vast majority of fabrics have what we call a right side (front), and a wrong side (back). The wrong side is recognizable because colors and patterns tend to be more faded or less clear. In plush it is the side without the hair. It is the side where we make all the mess: pattern marking, knots, and the ugly side of stitches. When you are done working on the wrong side, turn your little friend inside out to see the right side in all its splendor.

Some fabrics such as felt don't have a wrong and right side, so you have to choose a side to make marks and knots, and leave the other side clean. In some fabrics it can be unclear which side is the right and which is the wrong. In this case you may ask the seller to clarify it for you. Or, you can just choose the side you like the most. You might like the wrong side better than the right!

I will often say something like "right sides facing" or "right sides together," to indicate that two pieces of fabric should be put together facing each other (right sides hidden).

Allowances: Allowances are margins that we leave around the marked shapes on the fabric to avoid bursting the seams. I leave approximately half an inch allowance throughout the sewing process and trim it to around a quarter of an inch before turning the toy right side out. If you are working with fabric that has a high tendency to fray and unravel, don't do any trimming at the end.

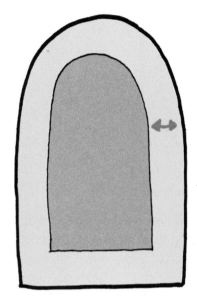

Allowances

Notching: Notching means cutting small "V" shapes in your allowance around curves after you sew them. This prevents wrinkling of the fabric.

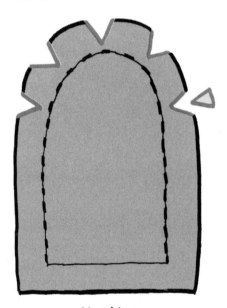

Notching

Appliqués: Appliqués are fabric shapes that are applied and sewn on top of other fabric shapes. In this book they are used for faces, features, and for ornamental purposes. They are generally made of felt.

Patterns

The patterns included in this book include a series of indications meant to make every step of the process as clear as possible. These indications are to be interpreted as follows:

Lines and Outlines

Black outlines are the regular shapes. You should mark them directly and leave half an inch of allowance when cutting the fabric around them. When you mark these shapes on fabric, be sure to leave some extra space around each of them for this allowance.

Pink outlines are for appliqués or loose shapes, this indication just means that you should not leave any allowance on these shapes. Cut your fabric following your marked lines as closely as possible. You can mark these on fabric without leaving much space between them.

Dashed gray lines are related to pattern assembly. They tell you that a shape is bigger than the sheet of paper that contains it, so the shape has been divided in two parts: the dashed line indicates where they should be put together before being glued to cardboard.

Dashed pink lines are suggestions for placing features and details.

Text Indications

The first line of text tells you the **name** of that shape so you can understand exactly what I'm referring to in the step-by-step instructions for that particular toy. The name may be followed by a **letter** between parenthesis; this is for shapes that are divided and need to be assembled. The letters indicate if it's the (R)ight, (L)eft, (T)op or (B)ottom part.

The second line of text indicates the **number of times that the shape needs to be marked** on fabric: x1 is one time, x2 is twice, and so on. If there are two numbers with a slash in between, it just means that you have to mark the shape the number of times the first number says, then turn the shape around and mark it "mirrored" as many times as the second number tells you to.

The third line of text indicates with an arrow which part of that shape is the **top**, since shapes can appear rotated for the purpose of fitting them on the page. I will sometimes refer to the "top" of a shape so this should prevent any misunderstandings.

Assembling the Patterns

The first step is scanning or photocopying the patterns for the plush toy you want to make. Cut around the shapes roughly, outside the lines.

If any of the shapes of your pattern are divided (marked by the gray dashed line on a border), cut along the dashed line closely, using the small solid lines as registration marks, and glue those pieces together.

Once you have all your shapes roughly cut, glue them (particularly around the outlines) to cardboard or thick paper. Try to use glue that doesn't buckle the paper. Once the glue dries, take your scissors and cut along the outlines of your shapes as precisely as you can. There you have it! Your patterns are now ready to be marked on fabric.

If you can print or copy the patterns directly onto very thick paper or thin cardboard, you may skip the "gluing to cardboard" step and just cut the printed shapes neatly from the beginning.

Marking the Fabric

To mark your patterns on the fabric, you must place the fabric you intend to use over a flat surface with the wrong side facing up. Place your pattern on the fabric, press it with your fingers, and draw carefully around it, as close as possible, with your preferred marking tool.

If you are using an ink-based tool (a marker or pen), always try it out on a border of the fabric to make sure it doesn't bleed.

If your fabric has a print, or if it has fur, pay attention to the direction of the print or the hair before marking it. For fur fabrics you'll want the hair going down, from the top of the shape to the bottom.

SEWING INSTRUCTIONS

Running Stitch

This is probably the most basic stitch of all. It's just the needle piercing evenly in and out of the fabric in a continuous line.

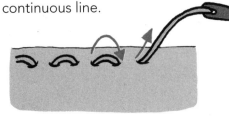

Running Stitch

There's a variation of this stitch where after you are done going forward with all your stitches, you go backward with a running stitch in the same line, covering up the spots you left open. (The front of the piece will look the same as the back.) This is called a **double running stitch.**

Backstitch

This one is a bit more complicated but still a very simple stitch. This is a very strong stitch and I highly recommend it for all internal or non-ornamental sewing. As the name indicates, for the backstitch you go back each time you make a stitch.

Starting from the left: Insert the needle from the underside of your material a bit to the left from your last stitch or knot and pull the thread. Go back to the left, to the point where your previous stitch is, and insert your needle from the top. Advance forward to the right, and insert the needle from the underside, a little to the right of your last stitch. Pull the thread, go back to the left and insert the needle from the top where your last stitch is, and so on.

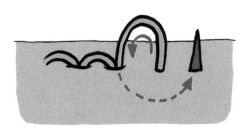

Backstitch

Whipstitch

The whipstitch is as simple as the running stitch but it advances sideways instead of forward, making the motion more like a zigzag.

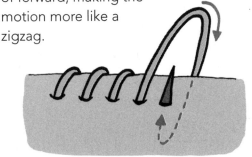

Whipstitch

Ladder Stitch

This is the stitch we use for closing the plush toys or when we don't want the stitches to be visible (which is why it's also called an invisible stitch). It's called ladder stitch because the shape the thread creates resembles a ladder.

To make this stitch you will need to fold the edges of your fabric and mark it a little so you will know where to make the stitches. The first knot, since you still have the hole fully open, should be made inserting the needle from the inside of the toy out, at the last stitch to the left of the hole. Insert the needle directly across the hole, in your marked fold in the other piece of fabric, from the front to the back. Pull the needle out on that same side of the hole, and then go directly across the hole again to the left side inserting the needle in your fold, from front to back, and repeat. Leave these stitches loose when sewing, and then pull the thread tight after every five or six stitches.

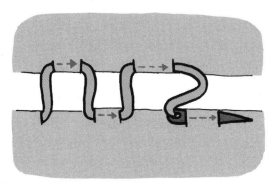

Ladder Stitch

Blanket Stitch

This is an external stitch and it's probably the most complex one used in this book. It takes a bit of practice to master. Once you get the hang of it, it looks great!

Joining two edges: Insert the needle from front to back (leaving some distance to the actual edges of the fabric), a little to the left of where you left your last stitch or knot, and pull the thread a bit until there's a small loop of thread left. Put your needle through that loop, back to front, and pull all the way. Insert your needle to the left again (at the same distance as before) again from front to back, pull a bit, put the needle through the loop, pull again, and repeat.

Appliqués: Insert the needle from front to back, leaving some distance to the border of the appliquéd fabric, a bit to the left of your last stitch or knot. Pull a little, and then pierce the fabric from back to front with your needle right above where you went in, at the very spot where the edge of the appliqué is, put the needle through the loop and pull. Repeat this process for each stitch.

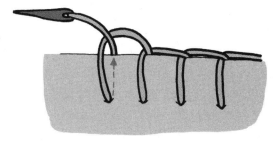

Blanket Stitch

Satin Stitch

This is a very useful embroidery stitch to fill areas. It consists of making long parallel stitches, one right next to the other, so there's no fabric visible between them, until you fill the desired shape.

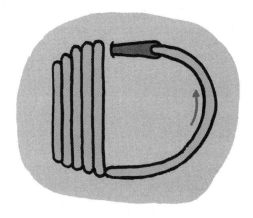

Satin Stitch

Tips for Hand Sewing

Wax: Waxing your thread with beeswax before you start sewing will strengthen it and make it less likely to snag or fray, and even if it does, it will be much easier to fix.

Hiding Your First Knot: When you sew on the right side of the fabric, such as when making a blanket stitch, we don't want the first knot to be visible. The best way to hide it is to "sandwich" it between the two pieces of fabric about to be sewn.

Hiding Your Final Knot: Whether you're using a ladder stitch for finishing up your toy, or an external stitch such as the blanket stitch, having the last knot showing never looks good, but luckily there's an easy way to hide it. Once you make your final stitch, make your knot. Then, push your needle through the seam (or as close to it as you can), squish your doll a bit and make the needle come out at some other random part of the doll that's not very close to the last stitch. Pull it firmly a couple of times, squish the doll again and cut the thread. All done!

Sewing Machine

Most of the instructions and tips in this book are aimed at hand sewing; since that's the way I've done the soft toys shown. But you can, of course, sew them using a sewing machine as well.

For the most part, you can follow the instructions directly, but replacing all mentions of backstitch with lockstitch, and all external and appliqué sewing with zigzag stitch or any other ornamental stitch that you like. Since the type and variety of sewing styles vary from one sewing machine to the other, you'll just have to be creative and choose the best one for each use!

However, it's important to note that many of the pattern shapes included in this book are somewhat complex, so if you're a beginner using the sewing machine, this may not be the best way to get started. You may want to practice first to make sure you can handle any shape. If you still wish to try it, I recommend using fabrics that are not thick or longhaired. You can always use a hemstitch on whatever you're about to sew just to be on the safe side. (A hemstitch is a running stitch made with long, loose stitches.)

SAFETY ISSUES   Making Plush Toys for Small Children

If your plush toy is going to be around small children, it's very important that you avoid including anything that can be easily pulled off. For features I recommend that you use child-safe eyes and noses. Each includes a shaft that punches through the fabric and is secured to a plastic piece from inside the toy, although you may want to glue them as well. You can get these at craft stores. Or you can sew on fabric features very tightly.

You shouldn't have any long shapes that may result in choking (such as long arms or tails, and accessories such as scarves or ties), or longhaired fur fabric on the toys. External sewing such as a blanket stitch should be avoided as well. Make your stitches as small, tight, and inaccessible as possible, and if you can, use a sewing machine for such toys.

Rod the Mouse

Materials:

Three kinds of fabric: Blue-green
and white felt and blue fleece
Thread: Brown and blue
polyester thread
Two eyes or buttons
Chalk marker (or any other
marking tool that doesn't bleed)

Scissors
Fabric glue
Stuffing
Sewing needle
Straight pins

Rod the Mouse

Rod is the nicest little mouse around! He likes tea and hazelnuts, and loves all things blue (like himself). This is probably the most basic plush toy in this book. It has a very straightforward process and a nice clean look. It gives you a basic understanding of what it takes to produce a simple soft toy.

- -

Step 1: Marking

Mark your patterns on the wrong side of the fabric with a chalk marker. The back and front of the main body and the two tail pieces are on blue fleece. The three stripes and two ear shapes are on green-blue felt. The face and tummy are on white felt.

Step 2: Cutting

The tail and main body shapes need half an inch allowance; the rest are all appliqués so you should cut them carefully along the marked lines.

Step 3: Face, Belly, and Stripes

Take one of your pieces of the main body; this will be the front of the doll. Place the face and tummy carefully where the pattern indicates, or a bit lower or higher if you feel like it.

Add a couple of tiny spots of fabric glue to prevent them from moving (you can also use a pin) and, with blue thread, sew around them with running stitch (*Figure 1*).

Repeat the process with the ear ovals, but sew them on with a whipstitch.

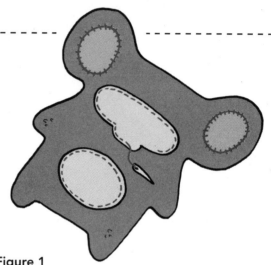

Figure 1

Take the other main body piece; this will be the back of the doll. Place, glue lightly, and sew on the three stripes using a whipstitch, in the same way you did with the ears. You will also find guidelines for their placement on the pattern (Figure 2).

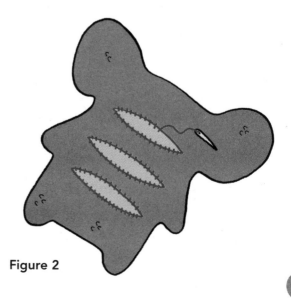

Figure 2

Step 4: Facial Features and Details

I used two shank buttons for the eyes. I didn't want them wiggling like they would if I just sewed them, so I cut a couple of small holes in the fabric of the face for those parts to go through and glued them onto the face (*Figure 3*).

I embroidered the nose and belly button onto the fabric using a satin stitch with polyester thread, but you can use embroidery thread if you prefer.

Figure 3

Step 5: Tail and Main Body

For the tail, take the two pieces of fabric right sides facing and pin them together. Sew around the piece following the marked lines with a backstitch, but leave the straight line on the top open (*Figure 4*).

Figure 4

Now turn the shape inside out. To make it easier, you can use the eraser end of a pencil to push the fabric. At the top of the tail (the open end) push a bit of the fabric in and close it using a ladder stitch. Attach the tail to the back of the doll using a whipstitch (*Figure 5*).

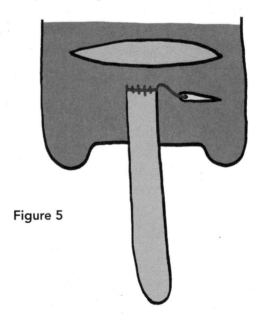

Figure 5

Now the front and back are now ready to be joined. For this we will repeat the process used for sewing the tail: pin the two right sides together (you may want to pin the tail rolled over itself for this step so it won't get caught in the stitches), and then sew following the lines using a backstitch. Leave the area between the legs of the mouse open for now (Figure 6).

Figure 6

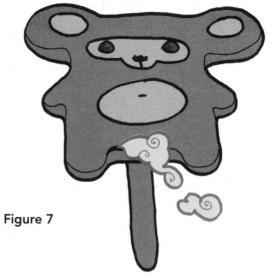

Figure 7

Once you're satisfied with how it looks and feels, close the hole with a ladder stitch and blue thread, and say hello to your new mouse friend!

This is a good moment to trim any excessive allowance you may have left. Then turn the doll inside out just like you did with the tail.

Step 6: Stuffing and Closing Your Plush Toy

Stuff your plush toy with polyester fiberfill, grabbing small pieces of it and pushing them through the hole. Fill the ears and limbs first, and then keep adding stuffing to the rest of the body (Figure 7).

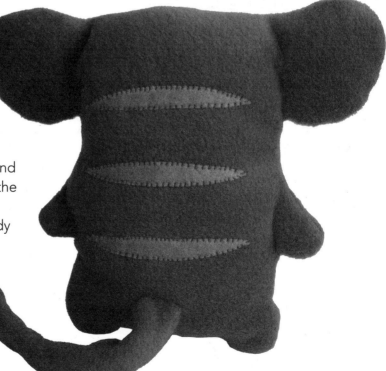

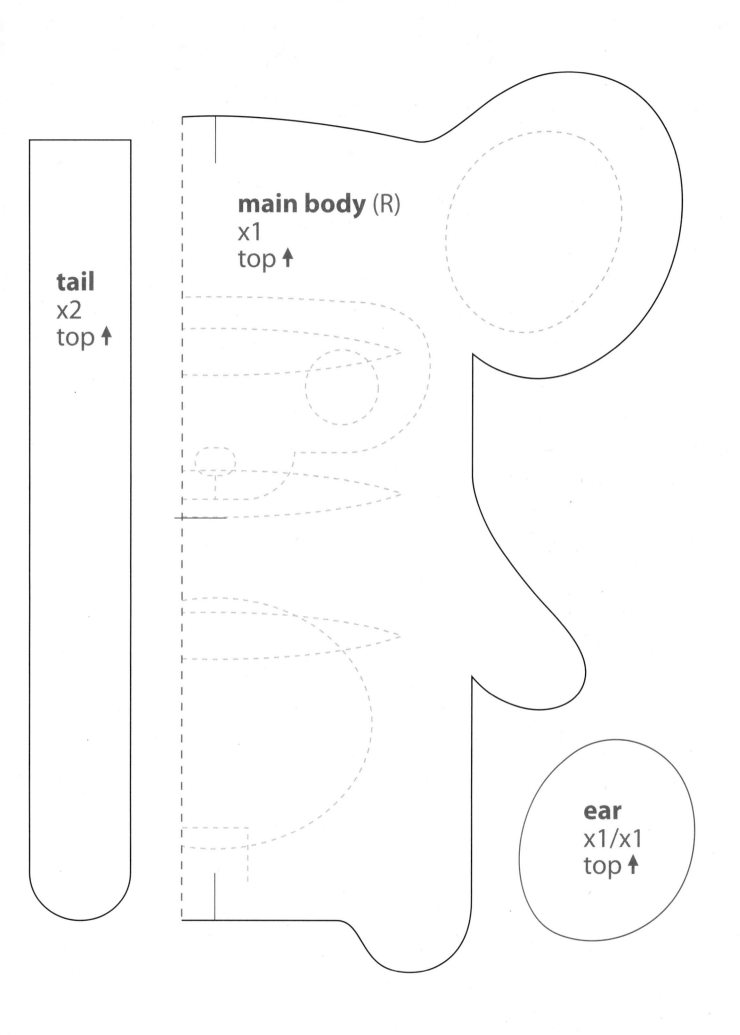

tail
x2
top ↑

main body (R)
x1
top ↑

ear
x1/x1
top ↑

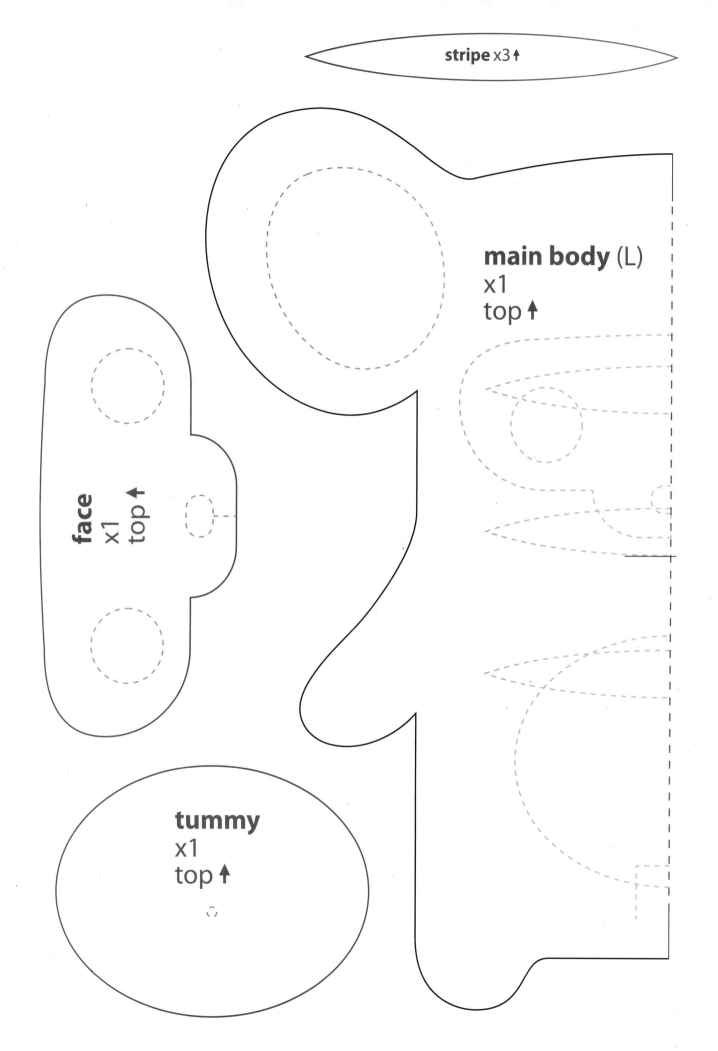

stripe x3 ↑

main body (L)
x1
top ↑

face
x1
top ↑

tummy
x1
top ↑

Little Lambert

Materials:

Three kinds of fabric:
Beige and black felt and light
ochre curly plush
Thread: Dark brown and black
polyester thread
Chalk marker (or any other
marking tool that doesn't bleed)

Two eyes or buttons
Scissors
Fabric glue
Stuffing
Sewing needle
Straight pins

Little Lambert

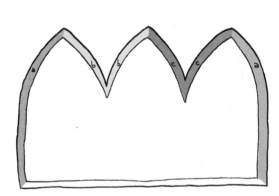

The sweetest and cuddliest of farm animals, Little Lambert loves the outdoors, fresh grass, and apple juice. Sometimes a wonderful fabric can be the inspiration for a creature, and when I saw this curly plush I just had to make a small sheep out of it. I created this fairly simple pattern, which produced a three-dimensional shape.

Step 1: Marking

Mark your patterns on the wrong side of the fabric with a chalk marker. I marked on the curly plush the main body, the bottom, two mirrored ears, the two shapes of the tail, the four parts of the arms, and four parts of the legs. On the beige felt I marked the face and the last two mirrored ears. On the black felt I marked the nose and the four hooves. Even if you've been using a different tool for the rest of the shapes, the hooves should be drawn with something that can be removed quite easily since you will see both sides of them in the final design.

Step 2: Cutting

The shapes with black outlines should be cut leaving around half an inch of allowance. The shapes with a pink outline (the face, nose, and four hoofs) don't need any allowance and must be cut carefully along the marked lines.

Step 3: Sewing the Main Body

The first shape we need to sew is the main body (*Figure 1*). This shape looks complex but it's actually quite easy and fast to sew.

Figure 1

Take your main body shape and fold it in half, right sides together, leaving only the wrong side of the fabric visible.

Check that the lines on both sides match and secure them with pins (*Figure 2*). Then sew along the side, joining the two borders labeled "a" in Figure 1, using a backstitch until you reach the top of the shape.

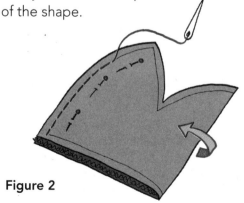

Figure 2

Take out the pins and join the other two smaller curves ("b" and "c") the same way as before to form the top of the head. First fasten the two pieces with pins then sew along the marked lines with a backstitch.

If you left generous margins in the previous step, you should trim them a bit now, as they may bulge later.

Step 4: The Face

Now that we have our main body put together, we are going to add the face. Turn your main body shape inside out to show the right side of the fabric, and flatten it on a table. Leave the long seam in the middle of the back. You should see two small seams at the top. Make sure these seams are the same distance from the edges.

With your felt face shape in hand, center it on the upper area of the main body, right below the ends of the small seams. Lift it a bit and put a couple of drops of fabric glue underneath, then press it. (You can secure it with pins if you choose not to use glue.) Once it dries, sew along the side, leaving a tiny margin to the edge, with a running stitch (Figure 3). Be careful not to sew through the back of the head. Remember to leave all of your knots on the inside of the shape.

Figure 3

Take whatever you've chosen to use as eyes and glue or sew them on the face. If you chose child-safe eyes or shank buttons, you will need to make little holes in the fabric with a cutter before attaching them. I've included dotted areas on the pattern to show you the placement I prefer, but you can put them higher or lower on the face if you wish (Figure 4).

Next step is sewing the nose. Place the shape right on the straight border in the middle of the face shape, as indicated in the face pattern by the dotted line. Add a drop of glue or pin it, and then secure it by sewing around the shape with whipstitch.

Figure 4

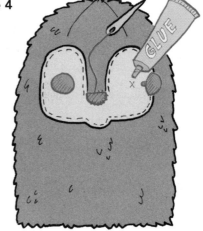

Last on our list is the mouth. You can stitch it or mark it with something easily removable. I used a double running stitch to do this, you can also use backstitch with similar results (Figure 5).

Figure 5

Step 5: Tail, Ears, Arms and Legs

The first thing we will put together is the tail, as it's the easiest of them all. Simply take both pieces of fabric, align them together with right sides facing, and sew around the U-shape with a backstitch, leaving the straight edge open.

The ears are done the same way as the tail except you will be sewing together two different kinds of fabric. Leave the straight edge of the shape open *(Figure 6)*.

Figure 6

You may want to notch the allowance around the ears and tail to prevent wrinkles at this point.

The process for the arms and legs is very similar. The only difference is that you need to place the hoof piece upside down at the bottom of the arm or leg between the two pieces of fabric, so that only the top edge shows (the two points should be hidden inside).

Figure 7

Then sew around the shape of the arm or leg with a backstitch, again leaving the top edge open *(Figure 7)*.

Last, you will need to turn all of these pieces inside out so the right side of the fabric shows. On the arms, you need to close the top edge with a ladder stitch. The same goes for the open side on each ear. You can leave legs and tail open, or just go over it with a quick whipstitch. I left arms, legs, ears, and tail empty, but you can stuff them a little before closing the tops if you choose to do so.

Step 6: Attaching Ears and Arms to the Main Body

We will now sew the ears and arms onto the sides of the main body. Attach the arms a short distance below the ears. Space them evenly from the face and the middle seam on the back *(Figure 8)*. It is not that important that you place the arms and ears where I have in terms of height, as long as each side matches. The ears and arms are attached to the body with a whipstitch (you can use a ladder stitch if you prefer the seams to be less visible). It's preferable to sew these by hand, not with a sewing machine.

Figure 8

Step 7: Sewing the Bottom, Legs, and Tail

First you need to turn the main body inside out. You should see the wrong side of the fabric for this step. Open the shape at the bottom, where there's no sewing done, and place the legs and tail inside. Align the top edges with the open border at the bottom of the main shape. The tail is positioned at the middle seam on the back of our creature and is secured with a pin. The legs should be pinned at the front of the toy about two inches apart (*Figure 9*).

Figure 9

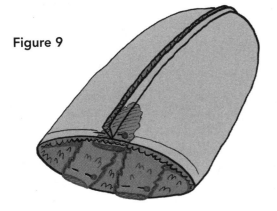

Next you need to sew the bottom to the main body, attaching the tail and legs in the process (*Figure 10*). Just place it covering the open bottom of the main body (again,

Figure 10

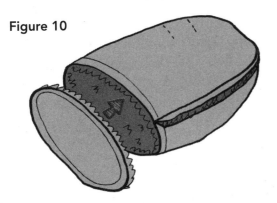

you'll be looking and working on the wrong side of the fabric). Start sewing a little before the tail with a backstitch and sew around the circle until right after you've attached the last leg, and make a knot. At this point you should notch around the main body and bottom seams. You should have a nice sized hole between the first and the last knot. Turn the toy inside out so the right side is showing.

Step 8: Stuffing Your Plush Toy

Stuff your plush toy with polyester fiberfill, grabbing small pieces of it and pushing them through the hole (*Figure 11*).

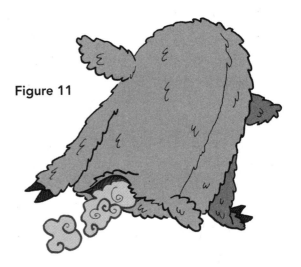

Figure 11

Once you're satisfied with how your toy looks and feels, close the hole with a ladder stitch and you're done! I hope you enjoy Little Lambert's company.

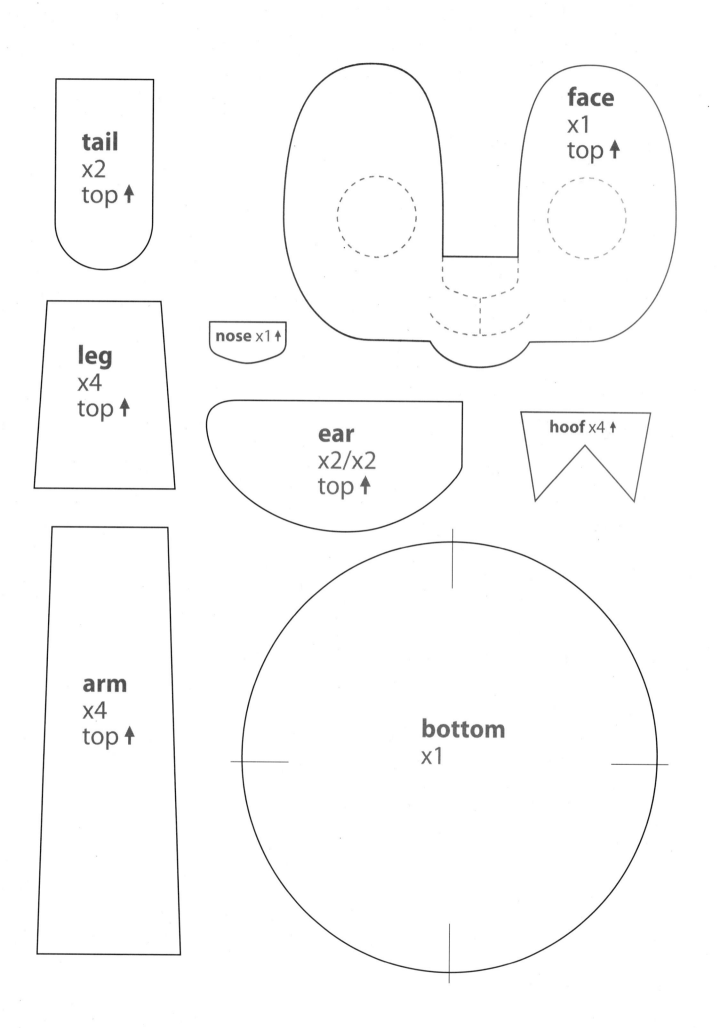

tail
x2
top ↑

face
x1
top ↑

leg
x4
top ↑

nose x1 ↑

ear
x2/x2
top ↑

hoof x4 ↑

arm
x4
top ↑

bottom
x1

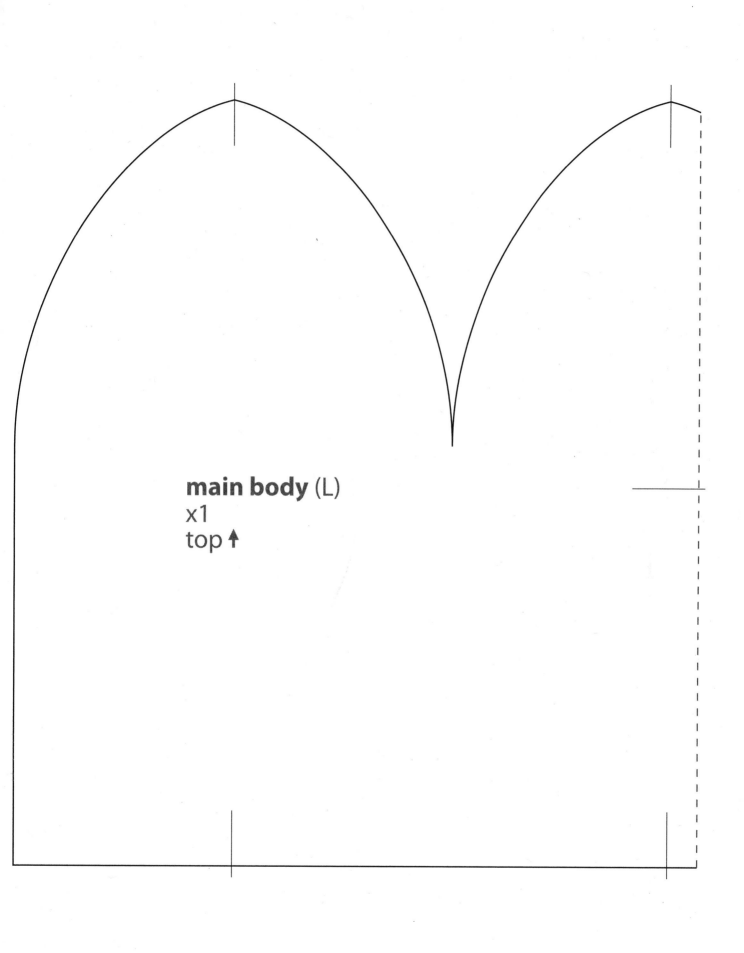

main body (L)
x1
top ↑

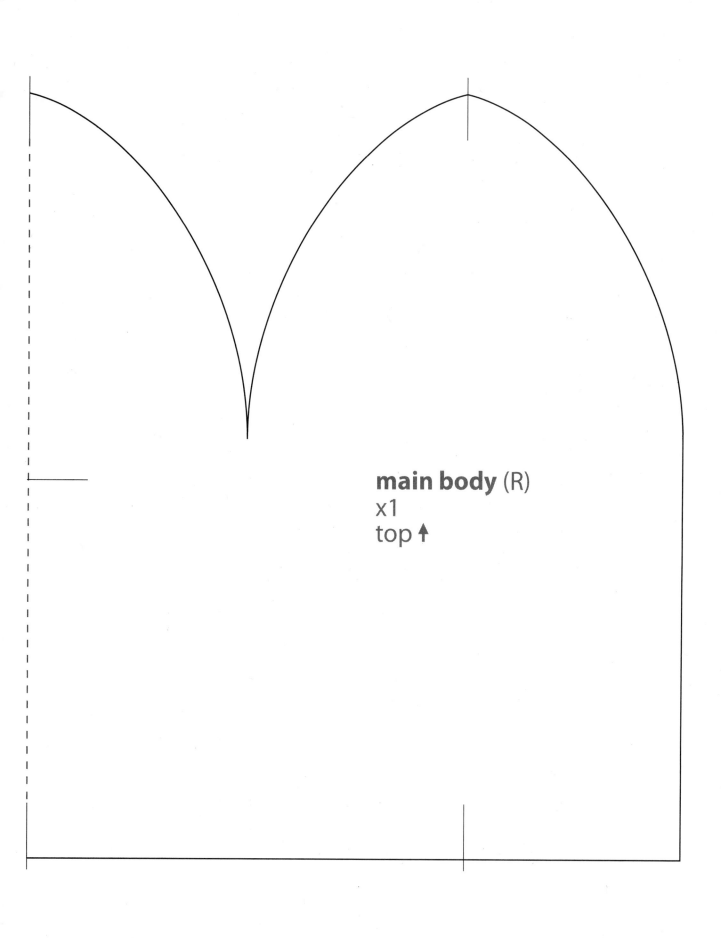

main body (R)
x1
top ↑

Cutecake

Materials:

Seven kinds of fabric: Fuchsia fleece, blue plush, black, beige, green-blue and pink felt, and cotton with a striped pattern
Thread: Blue, brown, and dark pink polyester thread

Chalk marker (or any other marking tool that doesn't bleed)
Scissors
Fabric glue
Stuffing
Sewing needle
Straight pins

Cutecake

A happy cupcake! You don't have to limit yourself to animals, and not even to living things, you can make an ordinary object come to life by turning it into one of our plush pals. The fact that Cutecake is not edible doesn't make our baked friend any less sweet for sure! This time we will combine different types of fabrics and colors so you can see for yourself how well they look and feel together.

Step 1: Marking

Mark your patterns on the wrong side of the fabric with a chalk marker. I marked the cherry on fuchsia fleece and the two eyes and the mouth are on black felt. The two cheeks are on pink felt. The cupcake liner is on beige felt, the frosting is blue plush, and the back silhouette is on striped cotton. There are some shapes, such as the frosting and cherry that include a series of small solid lines used as registration marks. Make sure to include these marks on your fabric, as they will come in handy later.

Step 2: Cutting

This plush toy is pretty tricky when it comes to cutting. You probably noticed this by looking at the outlines of your patterns. Some shapes, such as the cupcake liner and the cherry, have edges that you don't need to leave allowance for (solid pink lines) and edges that do require an allowance (solid black lines).

You will notice that there's no pattern marked on the green-blue felt that I included as a material, that's because with it you just need to cut, freehand, a strip around a quarter inch wide and 8 inches long, and divide that strip into small uneven pieces—that will be our cupcake's sprinkles. I chose not to include a pattern for this, as it looks better when they're not all perfectly alike.

Step 3: Assembling the Front Side

This step needs to be done pretty carefully. You need to refer to your pattern a lot. It helps having your back silhouette pattern around as well.

The "base" for assembling the front will be the frosting shape, and you will attach the cherry and the liner on top of it.

Place the cherry at the top of the frosting taking care that the markings you made match and that the point where your cherry stops having allowance aligns with the edge of the frosting shape. Take a close look at your patterns if you are unsure. Put a tiny bit of glue or pins where they overlap, and sew along the edge of the cherry where it is cut closely, using pink thread and a whipstitch (*Figure 1*).

With the liner on top, align the cupcake liner with the frosting and carefully check the marks on your pattern. Put a little glue or pins where they overlap. Sew the zigzagged edge with a whipstitch and brown thread.

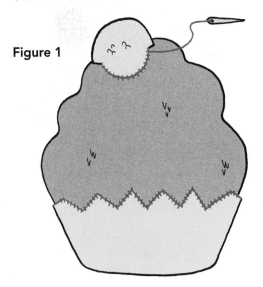

Figure 1

To make sure everything is sewn correctly, you can check the front shape against the back silhouette pattern to see if they match (Don't worry if there's a tiny bit of difference, this is normal and easily solved later on).

Step 4: Face, Sprinkles, and Other Details

Next we will make a face for our cupcake. This time we will apply the features directly onto the plush.

For this step you will need the shape you assembled in the previous step and all of your appliqués: eyes, mouth, cheeks, and sprinkles.

Place the black felt eyes and mouth onto the frosting in the desired position and glue them lightly or pin them (you can use the pattern as a guideline). Sew around the pattern with a whipstitch using black thread. Use this same technique for the pink felt cheeks, but use dark pink thread this time.

Randomly place the green-blue felt sprinkles on the frosting. Sew them on using a running stitch and blue thread.

The last stop for this step is detailing with thread. Make straight lines from the corners of your cupcake liner's zigzagged edge to the bottom with brown thread using a backstitch or a double running stitch (*Figure 2*).

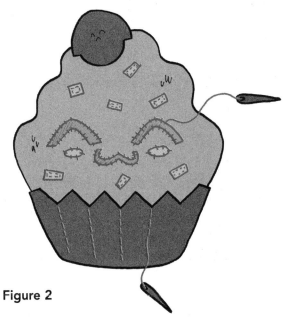

Figure 2

Step 5: Sewing Front and Back

All the hard work is done! Now it's time to put the front shape together with the back silhouette pattern with the right sides facing.

Sew all around the shape along your marked lines using a backstitch and brown thread. Make sure to leave an open space at the bottom to stuff it later (*Figure 3*).

Figure 3

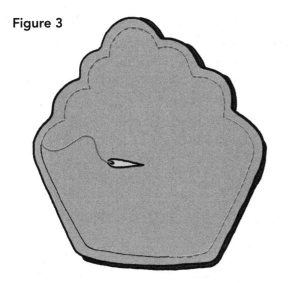

If the front and back have a small difference in proportion due to the assembling step, always follow the lines of your front shape. The allowance you left for the back silhouette pattern should cover any small mismatching more than enough. Once you have everything sewn together, you can trim the allowances if they're too generous.

Step 6: Stuffing and Closing Your Plush Toy

Stuff your plush toy with polyester fiberfill, grabbing small pieces of it and pushing them through the hole. Fill the cherry and all the rounded edges of the frosting first (*Figure 4*).

Figure 4

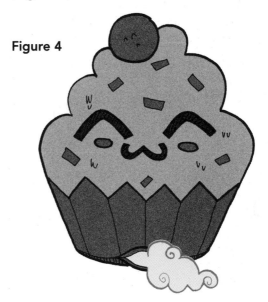

Once it's nice and round—but not bulging—close the hole using a ladder stitch and brown thread. Cutecake is now finished!

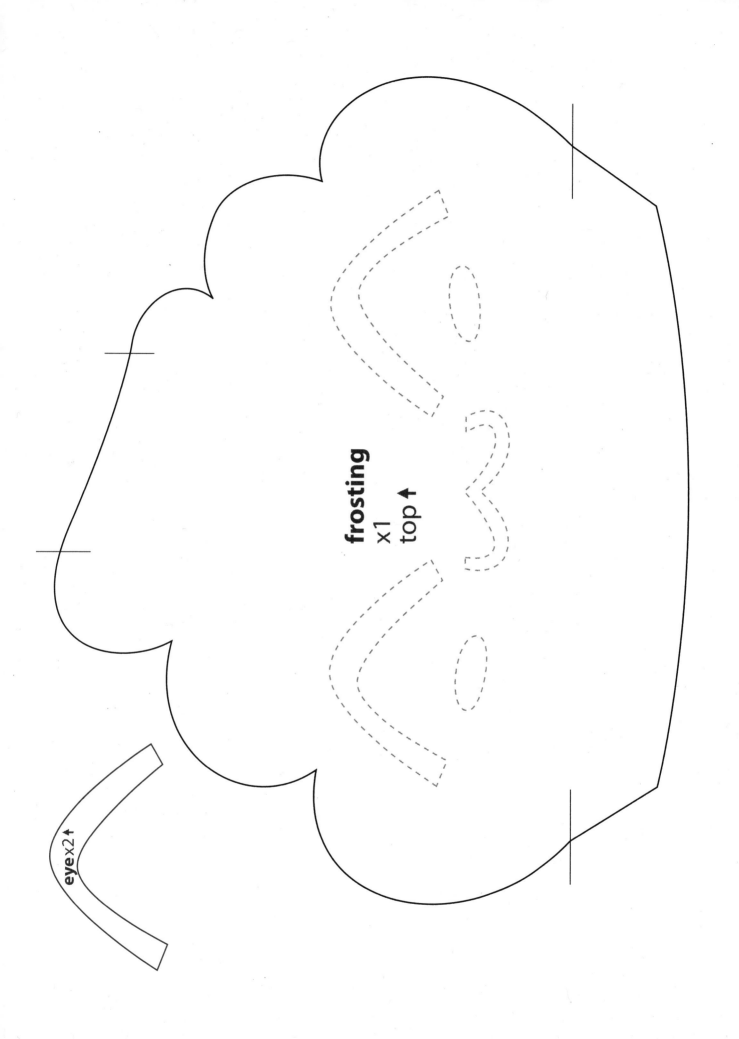

frosting
x1
top ↑

eye x2 ↑

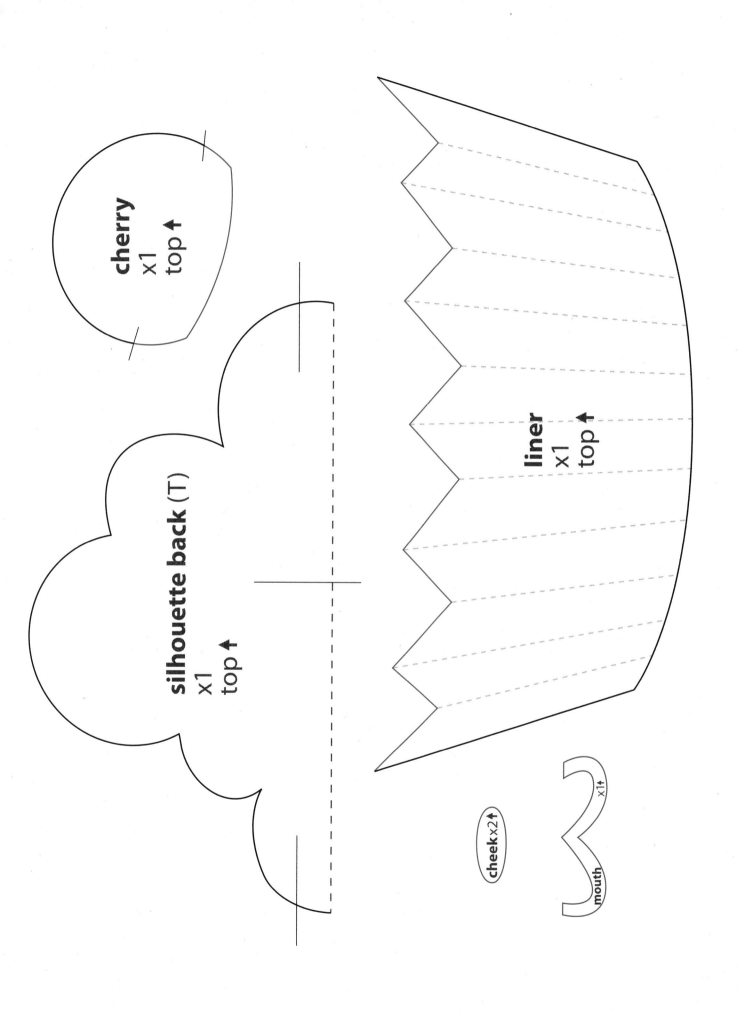

cherry
x1
top ↑

silhouette back (T)
x1
top ↑

liner
x1
top ↑

cheek x2 ↑

mouth
x1 ↑

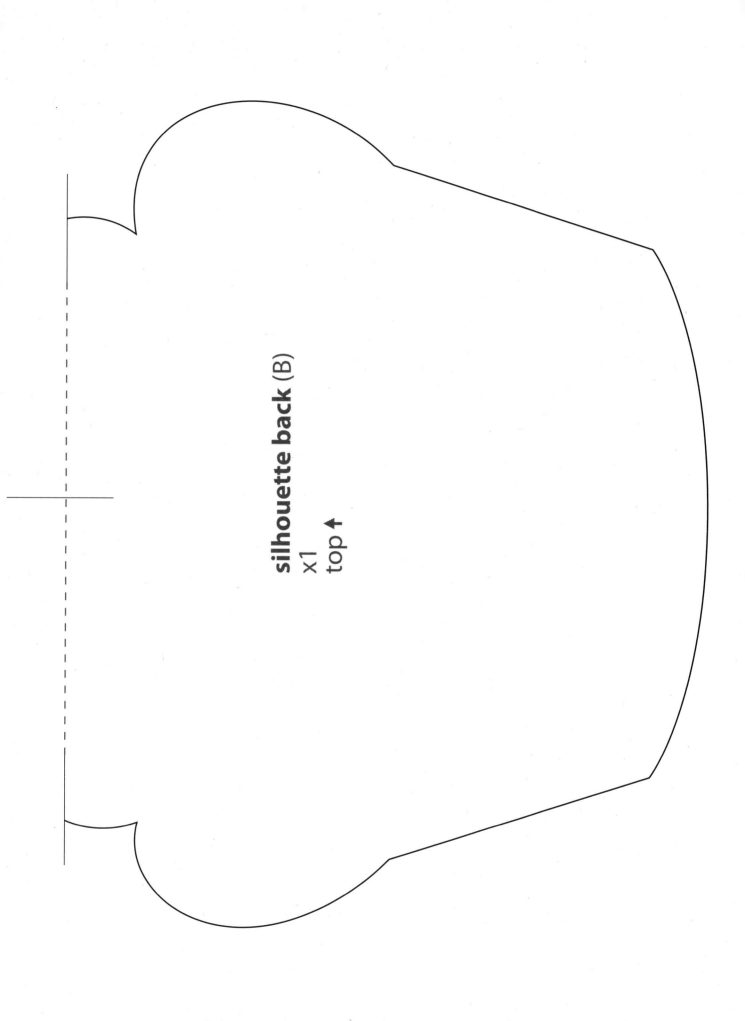

silhouette back (B)
x1
top ↑

Cubefish

Materials:

Three kinds of fabric: gray corduroy, blue-green and black felt
Thread: blue, black, and gray-green polyester thread
Two eyes or buttons
Scissors
Chalk marker (or any other marking tool that doesn't bleed)
Fabric glue
Stuffing
Sewing needle
Straight pins

Cubefish

Cubefish belongs to a rare species of aquatic geometric crafted creatures and is a very fun plush pal to make! As I mentioned previously in the "Fabrics" section, this is the perfect chance to use thick, rigid fabrics because, unlike most of our other plush creations, we don't want this guy to appear round when we stuff it.

Step 1: Marking

Mark your patterns on the wrong side of the fabric with a chalk marker. I marked on the gray corduroy the two top/bottom shapes, and the four front/sides/back shapes. On the blue-green felt I marked the two top fin pieces and the four side fins, as well as two tail pieces, the six scales, and the face. The mouth is marked on black felt.

Step 2: Cutting

You will need to leave allowance around all pattern pieces except the face, mouth, and the scales, which are indicated by solid pink lines.

Step 3: Face, Mouth, and Scales

You will need three of the front/sides/back shapes. One piece will be the front and the other two will be the sides of our cubic friend.

Take the one you chose to be the front and place the face on the right side of the fabric, apply a few drops of fabric glue to secure it in place (you can use pins instead) and sew around it using a running stitch and gray-green thread. Then place the mouth appliqué on top of it as shown in your pattern, and once again secure it with a bit of glue or pins. Sew the mouth onto the face using a whipstitch and black thread. Next, attach the eyes. I chose buttons for my Cubefish (*Figure 1*).

Figure 1

Now you can add some details to the face. You can copy the lines suggested in the face pattern or you can create your own. I marked the design very subtly with chalk and followed the lines with backstitch using blue thread. You can use embroidery thread for this if you want to make it stand out a bit more (*Figure 2*).

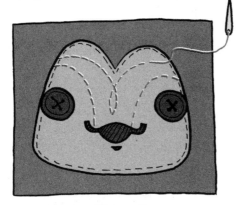

Figure 2

Put the finished face piece aside and take one of the two side patterns. Take three of the scales and sew the top of them in position using a whipstitch and gray-green thread. Don't sew the sides of the scales, just the top straight edge. Overlapping them a little in a sideways triangle arrangement as shown below (*Figure 3*). Follow the same procedure for attaching the scales to the other side shape. Make sure the scales on both sides of Cubefish are symmetrical.

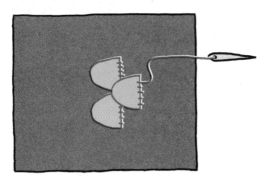

Figure 3

Step 4: Fins and Tail

Take your two top fin pieces, put the right sides together and sew around them using a backstitch and gray-green thread leaving the bottom straight edge open (*Figure 4*).

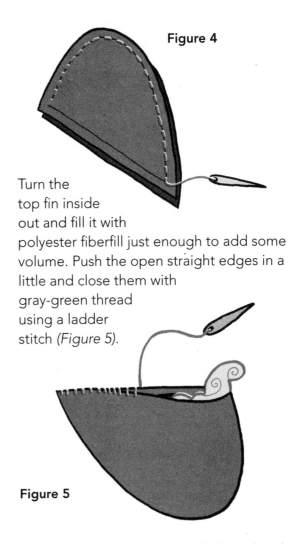

Figure 4

Turn the top fin inside out and fill it with polyester fiberfill just enough to add some volume. Push the open straight edges in a little and close them with gray-green thread using a ladder stitch (*Figure 5*).

Figure 5

Repeat the same process with the tail and the side fins, although you don't need a ladder stitch to close them. You can use a whipstitch since it won't be visible.

As you can see, the patterns for the fins and tail have a few pink dashed lines on them. These are rough guidelines for the details. Starting at the straight edge you sewed together, sew lines indicated in the pattern using a double running stitch (*Figure 6*).

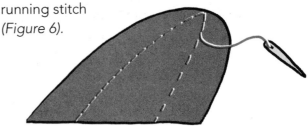

Figure 6

I used a double running stitch for this instead of a backstitch because both sides are visible (a backstitch only looks good on the front). We are using a double running stitch instead of a running stitch because it looks better and the beginning and end knots will be in the same place.

It's time to sew the tail to the back piece, and the top fin to the top piece. Place the straight edge of the top fin or tail centered on the appropriate piece. Attach them using a whipstitch and gray-green thread (*Figure 7*).

Figure 7

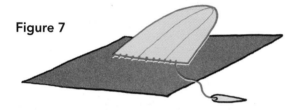

Step 5: Assembling the Body

This may seem a little complex at first, but you will see that it's actually not hard at all.

Attach the front piece with the face to all its adjacent shapes: sides, top and bottom. For this we will be using a backstitch and gray-green thread (*Figure 8*).

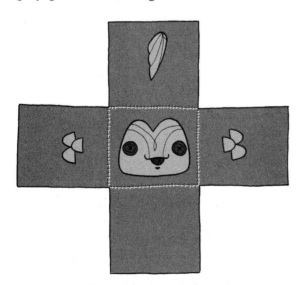

Figure 8

Sew the edges of the top piece to the sides, and attach the back piece to them as well using a backstitch and gray-green thread (*Figure 9*).

Figure 9

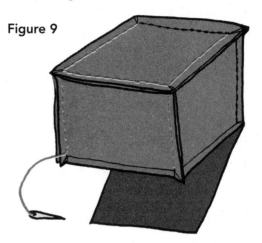

Attach the side fins onto the body by sandwiching them between the edges of each side rectangle and the bottom shape. Once they're in place, secure them with a pin and proceed to join the edges using a backstitch (*Figure 10*).

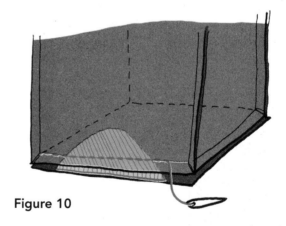

Figure 10

Join the back and bottom using a backstitch, but leave an opening in the middle for the next step—stuffing! Check that all the corners of the cube are tightly sewn and reinforce them with a couple of stitches if needed. Trim your allowances a bit if you must, then turn Cubefish right-side out.

Step 6: Stuffing and Closing Your Plush Toy

Stuff Cubefish using polyester fiberfill, grabbing pieces of it and pushing them through the opening you left in the back. There are no little limbs or parts here that need to be filled first so just stuff directly and evenly *(Figure 11)*.

Figure 11

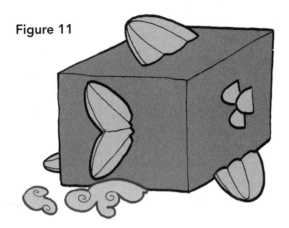

Once you're satisfied with how your plush toy looks and feels, close the opening using a ladder stitch and gray-green thread. Cubefish is now done!

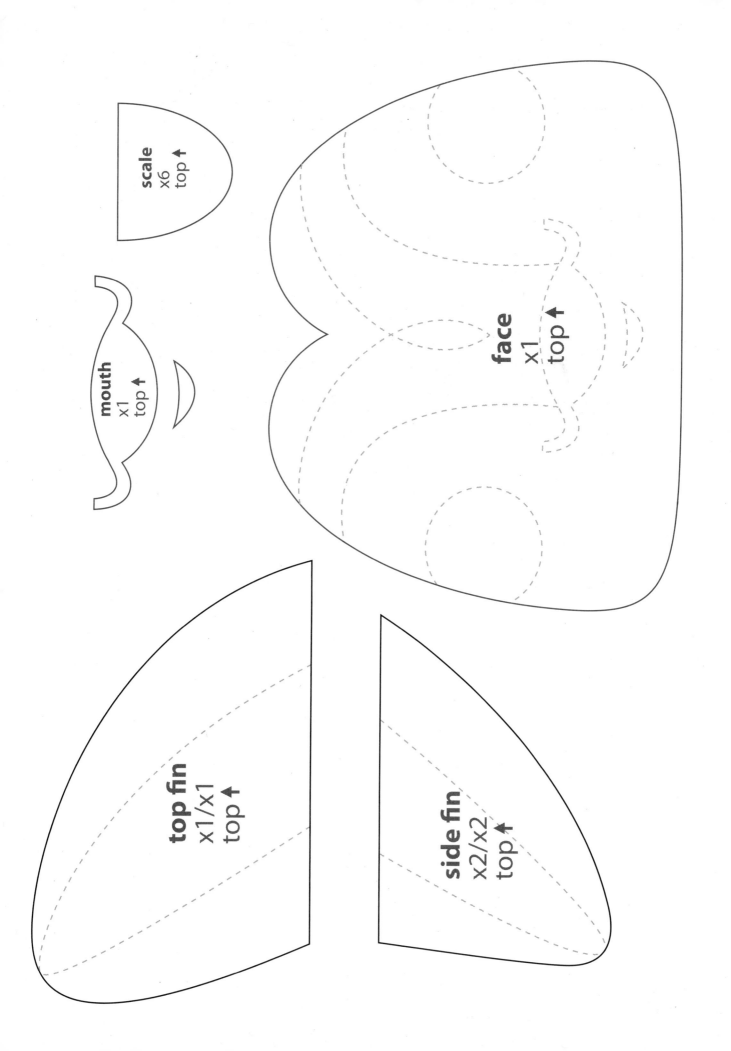

scale
x6
top ↑

mouth
x1
top ↑

face
x1
top ↑

top fin
x1/x1
top ↑

side fin
x2/x2
top ↑

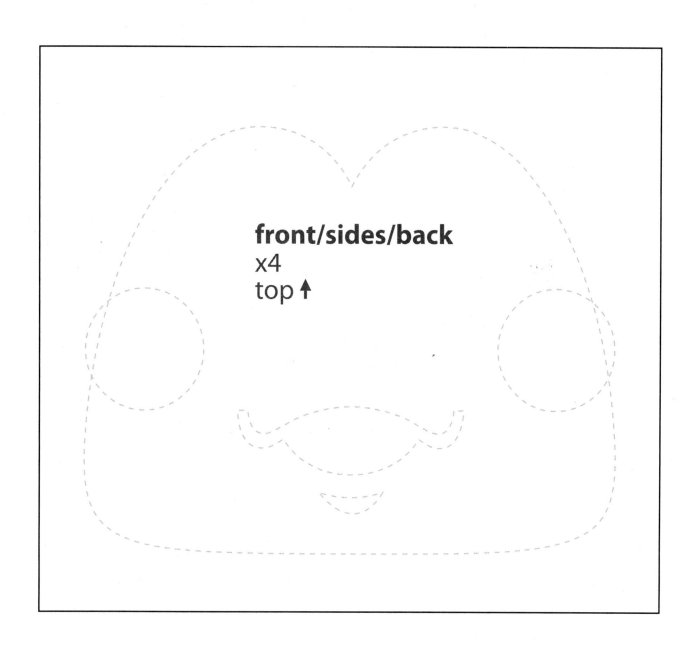

front/sides/back
x4
top ↑

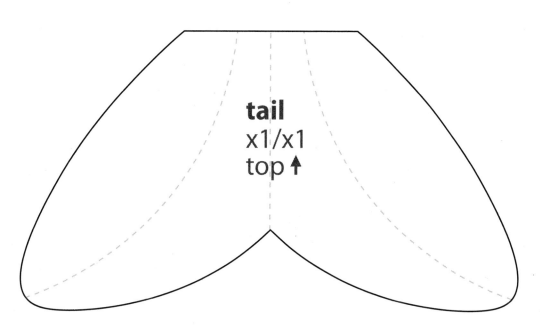

tail
x1/x1
top ↑

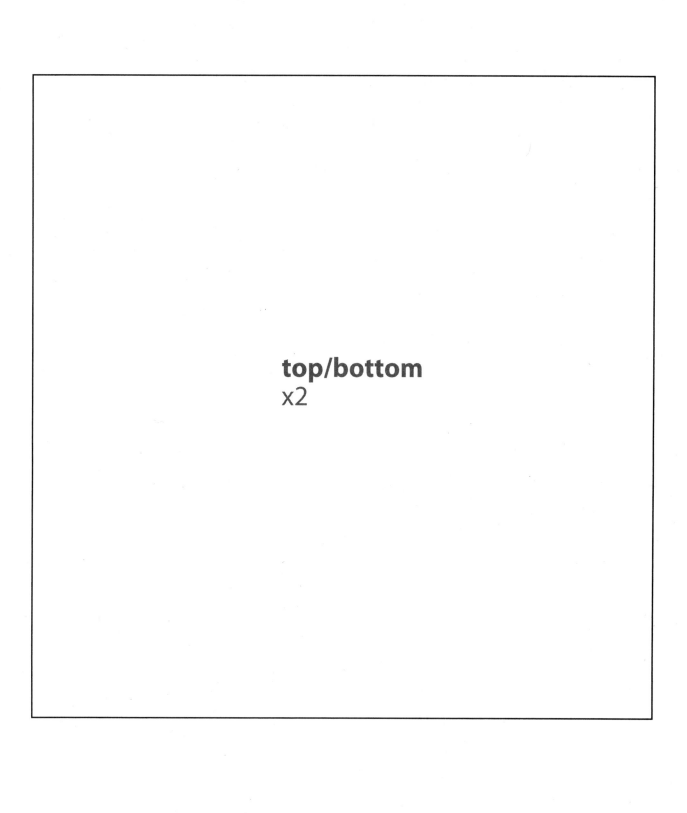

top/bottom
x2

Rosie the Strawberry

Materials:

Five kinds of fabric: Fuchsia and green fleece and pink, black, and blue-green felt
Thread: Blue-green, black, and dark pink polyester thread
Twenty small, transparent yellow beads

Chalk marker (or any other marking tool that doesn't bleed)
Scissors
Fabric glue
Stuffing
Sewing needle
Straight pins

Rosie the Strawberry

There's more than just animals in the Plush Pal universe... there's also fruit! This small strawberry loves all things pink and likes to smile a lot. For Rosie I wanted a very round shape so she's composed of many segments instead of just being front and back. It is also a good opportunity to include things besides fabric and thread, such as tiny beads, to add unique details to your plush toys and make them truly your own.

Step 1: Marking

Mark your patterns on the wrong side of the fabric with a chalk marker. I marked the four main body shapes on fuchsia fleece. The four leg patterns, the stem, and one leaf piece are marked on green fleece. The other leaf piece is marked on blue-green felt. The face is on pink felt, and the mouth and two eyes are on black felt.

Step 2: Cutting

Most of the shapes, except for the legs and the main body, don't need any allowance so they can be cut along the lines as indicated by the solid pink lines. Leave half an inch allowance for the legs and the main body shapes. If you're using fleece as instructed, you can trim it later in the process.

Step 3: Sewing the Segments Together

The main body has four segments. Take two of the segments, put them together with the right sides facing and sew one side

from top to bottom, leaving the other side open. For this use dark pink thread and a backstitch. Follow the same procedure for the remaining two segments *(Figure 1)*.

Figure 1

Take the two pieces and put them together, right sides facing, by separating the open edge on each. Align them carefully and sew one edge together from top to bottom exactly as in the previous step *(Figure 2)*. One edge is left open. Now turn the piece so you can see the right side of the fabric.

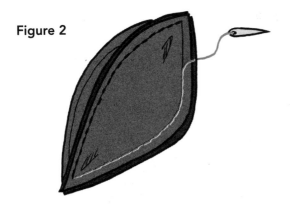

Figure 2

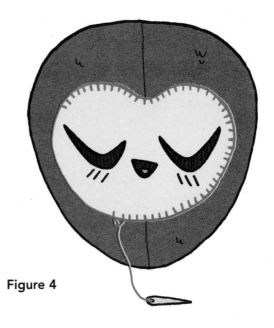

Figure 4

Step 4: The Face

Place the eye and mouth appliqués in position on top if the face pattern and secure them with in place with pins or a tiny bit of fabric glue. Sew around them using a whipstitch and black thread.

To make the tongue, apply pink thread using a satin stitch covering the bottom of the mouth appliqué. The cheeks are made with three long slanted parallel stitches (*Figure 3*).

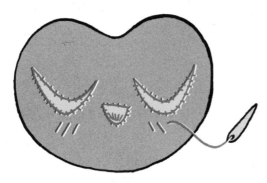

Figure 3

Take the main body shape and flatten the two continuous segments that are directly opposite to the edge you left open over a table. Center the face appliqué horizontally on the body using the seam as your guide and secure it with a bit of fabric glue or pins. Sew all around it using a blanket stitch (*Figure 4*).

If you don't have embroidery thread for this you can use two strands of polyester thread in your needle, even three, but I don't recommend more than that. The more strands you use, the more likely it can get tangled, so be careful.

Step 5: The Legs

The legs are pretty straightforward to make and if you've made other creatures from this book it should be a piece of cake. Take two mirrored leg patterns, put them together with the right sides facing each other, and sew all around them using a backstitch leaving the straight edge open for stuffing (*Figure 5*).

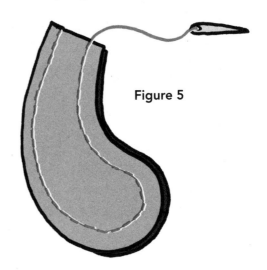

Figure 5

Follow the same procedure for the other leg pattern. Trim the seam allowance a bit if you left too much, and turn both of them right side out. You can use the eraser end of a pencil to help you out if needed.

Stuff both of the legs with polyester fiberfill, push their top edges in a bit and close them with ladder stitch (Figure 6). The legs are now done!

Figure 6

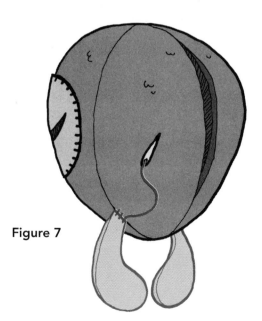

Attach each leg to the main body along the seams on each side of the face using a whipstitch and blue thread. Leave a distance of approximately two inches between each leg and the center seam at the bottom of the body (Figure 7).

Figure 7

Step 6: Detailing with Beads

Now we will add those little yellow seeds that strawberries have on their surface. For this we will use small transparent yellow beads. These have a little hole across them to be sewn down so I just attached them this way (Figure 8).

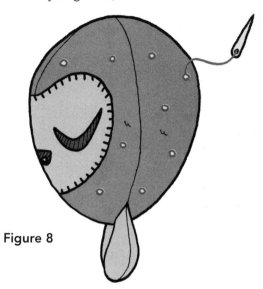

Figure 8

Try to spread them evenly on the whole main body, but don't include any on the face. I used approximately twenty beads for this toy, but if you want them to be more prominent you can use more. You might also want to try more brightly colored or opaque beads since the ones I chose are fairly transparent and not exceedingly noticeable.

Step 7: Leaf and Stem

For the stem, just fold the shape in half (follow the guideline in your pattern) hiding the wrong side of the fabric. Sew the open edge together using a whipstitch and blue thread (Figure 9).

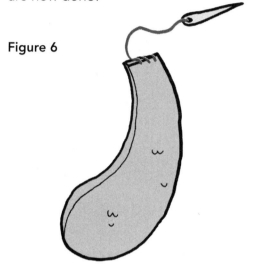

Figure 9

The leaf is easy to make. Just take your blue-green felt and green fleece pieces and put them together, but this time with their wrong sides facing. We will sew them together using a blanket stitch and blue thread. Make your stitches nice and neat, as you will be able to see them (Figure 10).

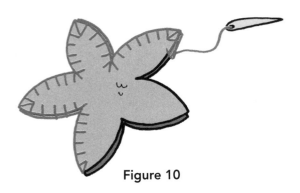

Figure 10

Attach the stem to the center of the leaf using a whipstitch and blue thread. Before we sew the leaf to the main body, we will need to close the opening we left in the back of the main body slightly. Turn the main body inside out so you can see the wrong side of the fabric and all the knots and mess. Sew along the open edge using a backstitch and pink thread a few inches from the top down and then a few inches

from the bottom leaving an open space in the middle (Figure 11). You can make a few extra stitches to secure the points where the four segments join, in the middle of the top and the bottom of the shape. These are critical spots and need to be sewn tightly so make sure there are not any loose stitches. At this point you can also trim any excess allowance you may have.

Figure 11

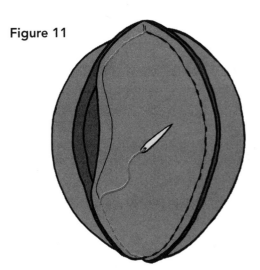

Turn the main body right side out and attach the stem and leaf to the top center point of the main body where all segments join (Figure 12). Sew only in that spot, where the stem can hide your stitches, using a whipstitch and blue thread.

Figure 12

Step 8: Stuffing and Closing Your Plush Toy

Fill your plush toy with polyester fiberfill, grabbing small pieces of it and pushing them through the opening on the back of the main body (*Figure 13*). Rosie the Strawberry needs to have plenty of stuffing to get really round, but don't overdo it! You don't want your seams bursting.

When you're happy with how Rosie looks and feels, close the opening using a ladder stitch and pink thread, and you're done. Enjoy your little strawberry creature!

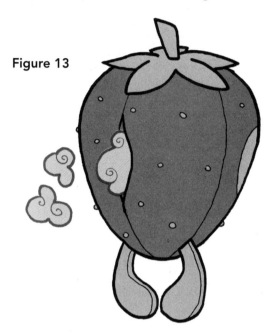

Figure 13

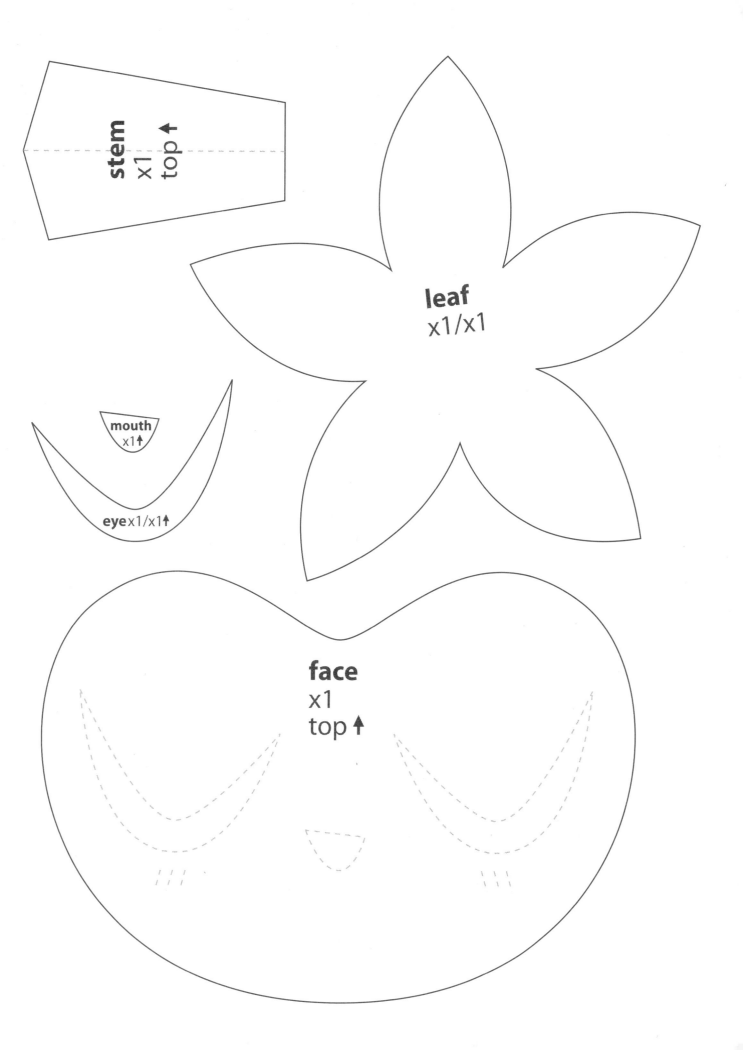

stem
x1
top ↑

leaf
x1/x1

mouth
x1↑

eye x1/x1↑

face
x1
top ↑

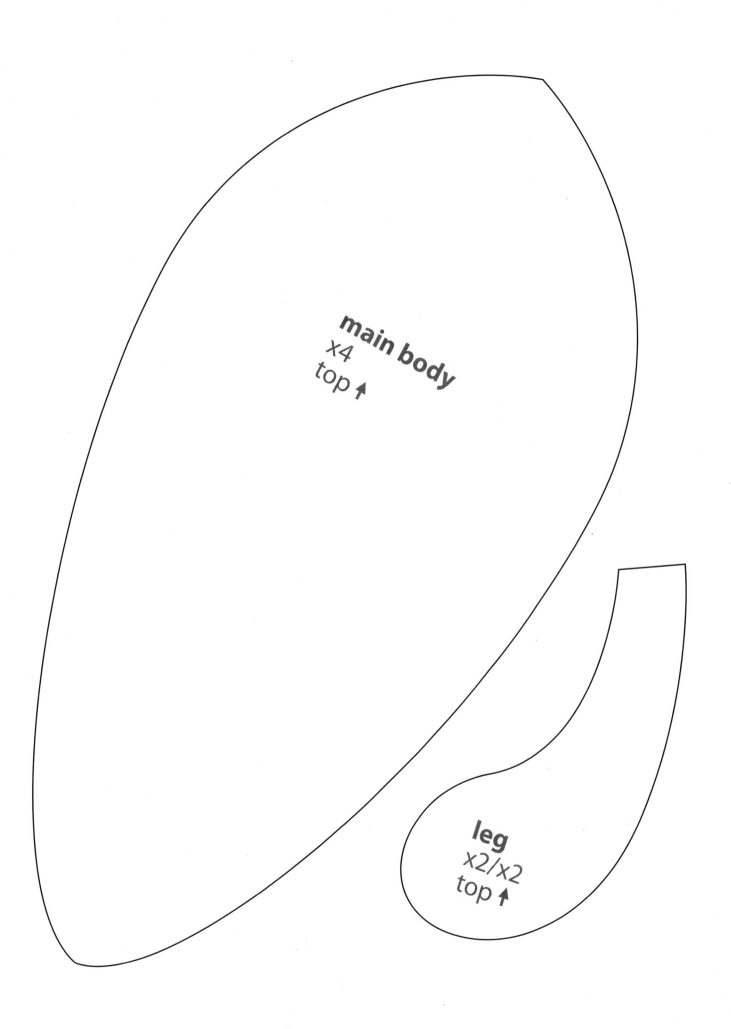

main body
x4
top ↑

leg
x2/x2
top ↑

Wingbunny

Materials:

Three kinds of fabric: Orange and blue fleece and white felt
Thread: Yellow and blue polyester thread and red embroidery thread
Two eyes or buttons
Scissors

Chalk marker (or any other marking tool that doesn't bleed)
Fabric glue
Stuffing
Sewing needle
Straight pins

Wingbunny

An orange bunny with long ears and short arms, this guy is a little weird but very lovable!

This time we will make the stitches an integral part of the overall final look of the plush toy by sewing it externally.

Step 1: Marking

Mark your patterns on the wrong side of the fabric with a chalk marker. I marked the two shapes of the main body and the four shapes of the arms on orange fleece. The face and the four wing shapes are marked on white felt and the stripes are on blue fleece.

Step 2: Cutting

This particular creature will be sewn externally, therefore you don't need to leave any allowance for any of the shapes, cut them all closely following the lines you marked.

Step 3: Face and Stripes

Take the front main body shape and place the face appliqué on top of it. You can use the placement suggested in the pattern or place it lower, but be mindful that you will also sew the arms in the front so leave some space for them. Put a tiny bit of fabric glue behind the face or pin it to the fleece, and sew all around it using a whipstitch and yellow thread.

Attach the plastic eyes or buttons on the face. You can place them wherever you want. I like how they look at the bottom of the face. Sew them if they're buttons or beads, pierce the fabric and secure them with the plastic ring if they're safety eyes, or glue them if they're googly eyes. The mouth of our bunny is a single straight line across the entire face appliqué just below the eyes. I used a backstitch with red embroidery thread (Figure 1).

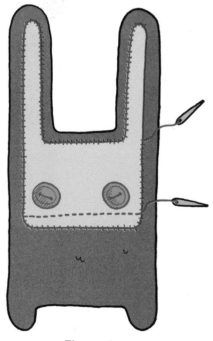

Figure 1

Now let's move to the back piece of the main body. Take your blue stripes, place them evenly on the back of the shape. Glue them lightly or pin them in place and proceed to sew them using a whipstitch and blue thread *(Figure 2)*. Don't worry if they're not perfect when comparing them with the pattern, these imperfections, most of the time, add a lot to the final look instead of detracting from it.

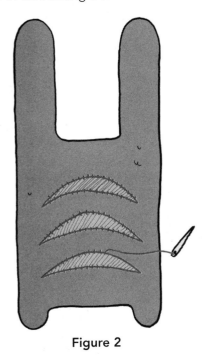

Figure 2

Step 4: Wings and Arms

The process is very similar for the wings and the arms. Let's start with the wings. Take two mirrored shapes and put them together, wrong sides facing. Since this time we will sew with a kind of stitch that's meant to show, we will be working directly on the right side of the fabric, unlike most of the other creatures in this book.

With the two wing pieces together, start sewing by the straight vertical edge you'll find on the side of the wings. Sew all around the shape using a blanket stitch and blue thread; end on the straight edge where you started *(Figure 3)*.

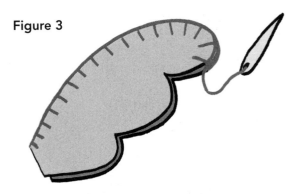

Figure 3

For the arms, the process is pretty much the same. Put the two arm shapes together, wrong sides facing, and sew around the edges using a blanket stitch and red thread. I used embroidery thread for this since it pops out more. Start sewing on one of the corners by the straight edge. Sew all around the arm; once you reach the opposite side of the straight edge attach the arm to the main body using the same blanket stitch and thread *(Figure 4)*.

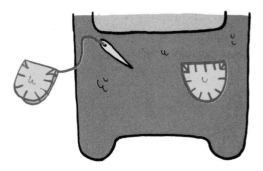

Figure 4

Step 5: Sewing the Main Body

Now that you have everything ready, put your front and back shapes of the main body together, wrong sides facing. Align them carefully and put the wings into each side of the creature. The straight edge should be sandwiched between the two pieces of fabric of the main body. Put some pins here and there to secure all the pieces. Proceed to sew all around the bunny with red thread using a blanket stitch leaving the space between the legs open to stuff it later *(Figure 5)*. There's no need to knot and cut the thread. Just leave the needle and thread there to continue sewing after the toy is stuffed.

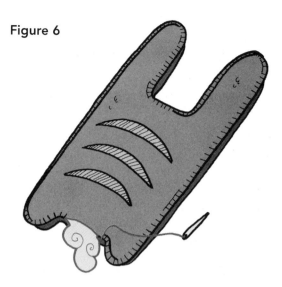

Figure 6

Figure 5

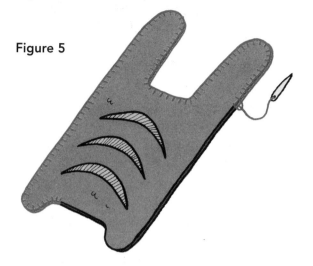

Once you're satisfied with how it looks and feels, close the hole by continuing the blanket stitch you were sewing before. And you're done!

Step 6: Stuffing and Closing Your Plush Toy

Put small pieces of polyester stuffing through the hole you left between the bunny's legs (*Figure 6*). Take care to fill the ears and legs well before filling the whole body. You can use the eraser side of a pencil to help get the stuffing into small areas. Don't overstuff it!

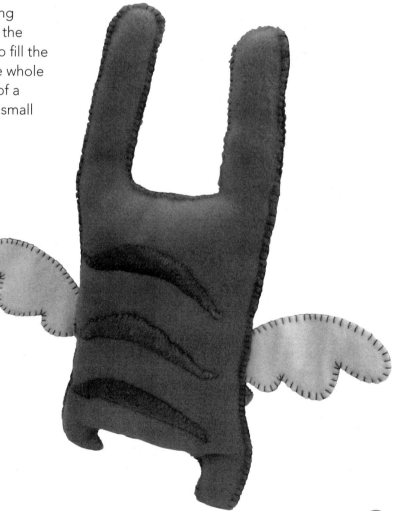

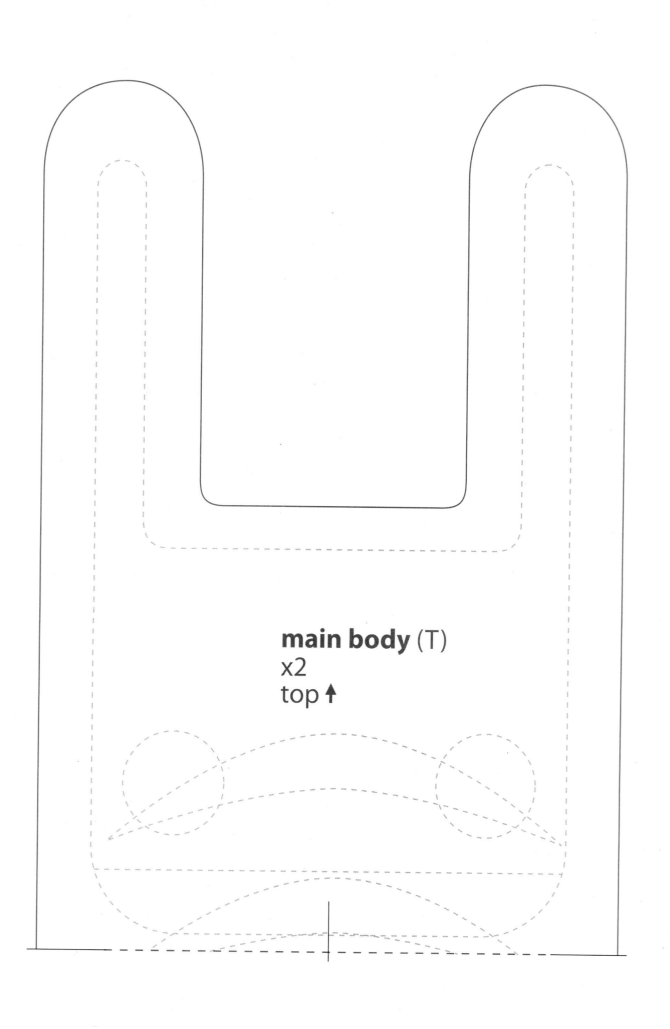

main body (T)
x2
top ⬆

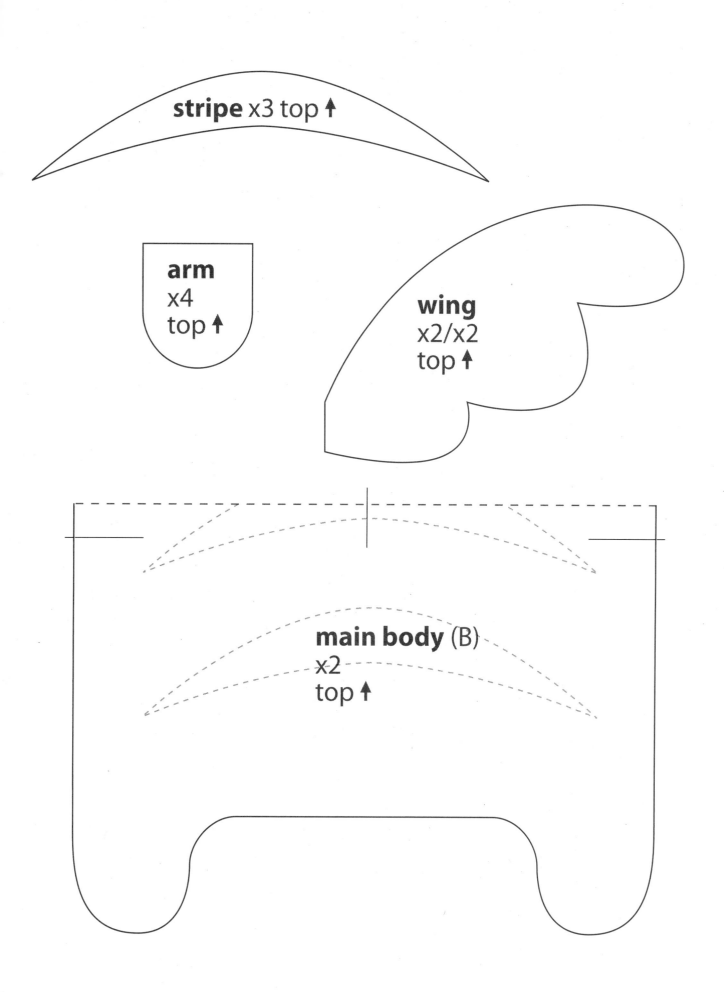

stripe x3 top ↑

arm
x4
top ↑

wing
x2/x2
top ↑

main body (B)
x2
top ↑

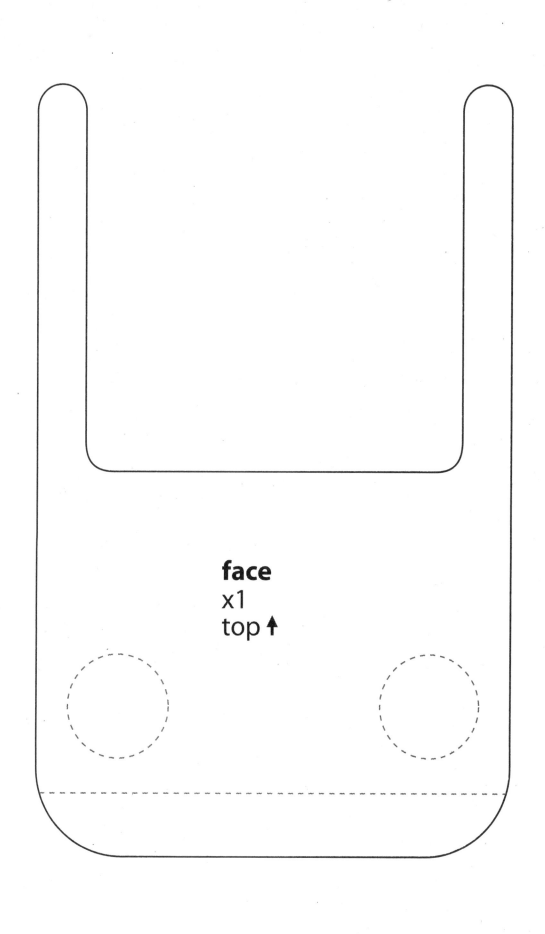

face
x1
top ↑

Customizing Your Plush Pal

Following instructions and getting the desired results are great, but making your creations unique and interesting is even more fun! So, I decided to put together a few tips and ideas—some super simple and some complex—for you to make your plush creations your own and get your imagination running wild.

Props and Accessories

The first and easiest way to add that little extra touch to your soft toys is adding accessories. Many craft stores carry things such as small straw hats, wire glasses, fake flowers, headbands, and wigs. You can also buy a variety of eyes and noses and snouts and use those instead of the ones I suggested. Sometimes you can even find plastic or wooden objects and furniture for your creations.

Adding ribbons and lace or making felt accessories for appliqués are also good options. Try making flowers, stars, hearts, mustaches, big eyebrows, and eye patches for your plush toy.

You saw how we used beads on Rosie the Strawberry to give it some texture—you can also use beads for giving your plush toy freckles. Make a necklace or armband with the beads to put on your little fellow. You can also create patterns or drawings with them on the surface of your fabric. Try using ornamental buttons—there are a huge variety of shapes and colors you can choose from.

Just like with beads, you can use fabric to create texture. The scales that Cubefish has, for instance, can be repeated to cover the whole surface of the fabric. You could make them feather-shaped as well. Other options for adding texture are felt balls or sequins.

Making Use of Your Skills

You don't have to limit yourself to bought items or simple additions—there are endless possibilities of what you can do. If you have any additional skills you can make use of them to make your projects all the more interesting.

Being skilled in embroidery means that you can add all sorts of patterns, not only on the faces, but on every surface of your plush toy! Take, for instance, Wingbunny or Rod the Mouse. You could make the stripes embroidered instead of appliquéd. Or, you could embroider those mustaches and eyebrows I mentioned earlier.

If you know how to sculpt, cast, or model, you can make your own eyes, beaks, paws, snouts, or any other part or accessory you can think of and add it to your creature.

Clay, resin, cold porcelain, papier-mâché—choose your medium and start creating!

If you're skilled at painting, or you know silkscreen printing (or any other way to transfer drawings to fabric), you can add your own facial features and details graphically instead of using fabric or other materials. You can also paint or print different motifs in your fabrics. For example, those yellow dots on Rosie can be painted with puff paint instead of sewing beads.

If you know how to knit or crochet, you can make scarves, hats, gloves, clothing or accessories. You can make the shapes of the patterns or the appliqués knitted or crocheted instead of using fabric.

There are probably many other skills and their possible applications that I'm overlooking, but this is just to give you a general idea of how many different ways you can personalize your plush toys. Do you like needle felting? Straw plaiting? Woodcarving? Anything goes!

Mixing and Matching

Now, when it comes to modifying the actual creature and not just its details, the easiest way to start is mixing and matching. Mixing and matching what? The different patterns you have here, of course!

Let's say you want a fish creature, but you don't want it to be cube shaped. How about using the main shape for Rosie the Strawberry, and adding the fins and tail of Cubefish?

You could do a cube-shaped strawberry by making the cube red and adding the leaf, stem, and yellow dots from Rosie's design to it.

Using Lambert's main shape and bottom and making six or eight tails from Rod the Mouse, you could make an octopus creature.

Rosie's legs can make antlers on top of Lambert's head.

You could also use Rosie's legs and Wingbunny's arms, or Lambert's tail on Cutecake.

The wings on Wingbunny could be used on any other creature to make winged versions of them.

You can turn around Wingbunny's main shape and make a creature with long legs and short ears.

Faces and features of all your creatures can be easily interchangeable.

Modifying Your Patterns

Of course, mixing and matching is just the tip of the iceberg. By using the patterns and making small additions (or subtractions), you can create totally new shapes.

You can add length and width to your patterns by marking part of it on the fabric, moving the pattern, and marking some more. This way you could make a much wider Wingbunny or one with very long ears.

A more complex example: Draw a horizontal line in the middle of your Lambert's body and take out the lower rectangle, add a few legs to the mix (Lambert's tail, Wingbunny's arms, and Rosie's stem are a few shapes that come to mind for this) and make yourself a ladybug or a spider. You could draw a U-shape and mark it twice to add wings to make a fly.

Stretch or squash your strawberry's main body shape by marking the upper half of your pattern on the fabric, slide the shape up or down a little, and continue marking. This can make more rounded or longer shapes that are perfect for making a whole family of other fruits. The squashed one is perfect for an apple, and if you turn the stretched one around and you can use it to make a pear or a fig. Remove the star-shaped leaves and use just the stem with a normal leaf attached to it and you'll get the full effect.

You can transform Cutecake into an ice-cream plush pal if you continue the sides of the liner all the way down and finish it with a V-shape, and change the zigzag edge to a continuous one.

If you mark Lambert's body, turn the pattern upside down and continue marking from the bottom, you'll get a long shape with both sides rounded—perfect for a worm plush toy! You can add some wings to it and a few legs and make a butterfly too!

Making Your Own Patterns

What about making your own patterns and designs from scratch? Well, even though this is quite a different animal that could probably use a whole book of its own, there are some things you can start with when it comes to creating your own plush pals.

The easiest kind of creature you can create are the ones with only front and back shapes to their main bodies (such as Wingbunny, Cutecake, or Rod the Mouse). You can draw any kind of shape, freehand or not, even if it's not symmetrical, mark it, turn it around and mark it "mirrored" again,

sew both pieces together and you're done. Any silhouette you can think of will work for this, and you can always add details, limbs, features, or anything you like to make it more appealing.

For more three-dimensional shapes, things get more complex, since there's not just one way to approach this, and it all depends on what you want to achieve. Regardless, there are some basic ways to make your shapes more volumetric:

If all you want is to give some volume to a silhouette, the simplest of solutions is adding a strip of fabric of any width you want between front and back shapes. If you make it really, really wide you get a cylinder kind of effect (depending on the shape) that works great for more three-dimensional limbs.

Another good way to generate roundness is darts: making V-folds on the edges of your shapes and sewing them. The rounded shape of Lambert's head is accomplished in a similar manner, although in that case the excess fabric from the dart is already removed in the pattern stage.

You can also create volumetric shapes by dividing symmetrical shapes in two and curving the resulting straight edge out. For example, let's say you have a pear shape. Draw a vertical line across the middle of it. You will need only half the pear as pattern, so erase the other one. Transform that vertical line you drew into a curve so it bulges out a little. Combining this shape with its "mirrored" version will result in the same pear shape you had at first but with a lot more volume.

You can combine these basic solutions in different manners, and there are many, many more. Whenever I'm unsure of how a shape will work, I make very rough prototypes with fabric leftovers to see if I'm heading in the right direction, then I make small adjustments to my design.

Of course, patterns are not absolutely and strictly necessary. There are a lot of crafters that don't use them for their creatures, choosing a more intuitive and improvisational process instead. I have never tried this particular method so I can't give much advice on how to approach it, but it's definitely a valid option if you wish to try it out.

In any case, patterns or not, the more complicated the idea for plush toy is, the more knowledge you'll need to pull it off successfully. You can gain the knowledge by means of prototyping, trial and error, and by doing tons of research, which brings us to our next topic.

Research, Research, Research!

As extensive as I may try to be in my explanations and instructions, the truth is that my sole experience is always going to be limited and probably insufficient to cover all of your doubts, but don't worry! There's a whole world of resources out there to explore.

Not only are there an incredible number of books and magazines on everything craft and toy related, which you can buy or check out in libraries and bookstores, there's also a vast amount of information to be found online. From sewing instructions and other embroidery stitches, to toy patterns, useful tips and most importantly, tons of inspiration, the web is certainly one of the most complete resources you will find when it comes to tutorials and learning new methods for making even more fantastic creations.

I have learned a lot from reading blogs, watching videos, checking out communities, and admiring other creator's handmade products.

There are also many shops (online or otherwise) where you can buy fabrics, stuffing, vintage buttons, safety eyes, and other cool items. Many craft stores also hold courses or classes where you can learn new things to apply later in your endeavors.

Another great way to find out more about plushie making is observing other people's creations and analyzing them, checking where the seams are, what kind of materials they use, thinking what is it about that design that makes it special. You can also get one of those super cheap soft toys that you can buy at supermarkets or malls to take it apart and see how it was made. If you feel sorry for the poor fellow you can always sew him back together.

If your goal is to make all those wonderful ideas you have come to life, and even take them further, the key is to keep yourself interested, learn new things, and try them out.

About the Author

Victoria Maderna is an Argentinian illustrator who loves to draw cute animals and other funny creatures. One day she decided it would be fun to make a plush toy out of one of her doodles for a friend, so she bought some fabric, thread, buttons, and stuffing and got all of her fingers pricked with the needle, but succeeded. Her friend loved the plush toy! And when she posted some pictures on the Internet, she got such positive feedback she thought it would be a good idea to make some more. After that she proposed making this book to help other people make their own stuffed creatures to give as gifts, trade them, sell them or just for plain fun!

DOVER CRAFT BOOKS

BASIC BOOKBINDING, A. W. Lewis. (0-486-20169-4)

CLOISONNÉ ENAMELING AND JEWELRY MAKING, Felicia Liban and Louise Mitchell. (0-486-25971-4)

BOOMERANGS: HOW TO MAKE AND THROW THEM, Bernard S. Mason. (0-486-23028-7)

JEWELRY MAKING: TECHNIQUES FOR METAL, Tim McCreight. (0-486-44043-5)

MAKING BEAD JEWELRY AND DECORATIVE ACCESSORIES, Virginia Nathanson. (0-486-44286-1)

NEW PATTERNS FOR BEAD FLOWERS AND DECORATIONS, Virginia Nathanson. (0-486-43297-1)

BOUQUETS FROM BEADS, Virginia Osterland. (0-486-43545-8)

JEWELRY MAKING FOR BEGINNERS: 32 PROJECTS WITH METALS, Greta Pack. (0-486-46041-X)

HOW TO MAKE MISSION STYLE LAMPS AND SHADES, Popular Mechanics Co. (0-486-24244-7)

1001 SCROLLS, ORNAMENTS AND BORDERS: READY-TO-USE ILLUSTRATIONS FOR DECOUPAGE AND OTHER CRAFTS, Edited by Eleanor Hasbrouck Rawlings. (0-486-23795-8)

EASY-TO-MAKE DECORATIVE PAPER SNOWFLAKES, Brenda Lee Reed. (0-486-25408-9)

OLD-FASHIONED RIBBON ART: IDEAS AND DESIGNS FOR ACCESSORIES AND DECORATIONS, Ribbon Art Publishing Company. (0-486-25174-8)

JEWELRY MAKING AND DESIGN, Augustus F. Rose and Antonio Cirino. (0-486-21750-7)

HAND PUPPETS: HOW TO MAKE AND USE THEM, Laura Ross. (0-486-26161-1)

PRACTICAL AND ORNAMENTAL KNOTS, George Russell Shaw. (0-486-46020-7)

CLASSIC WROUGHT IRONWORK PATTERNS AND DESIGNS, Tunstall Small and Christopher Woodbridge. (0-486-44364-7)

EASY-TO-MAKE STORYBOOK DOLLS: A "NOVEL" APPROACH TO CLOTH DOLLMAKING, Sherralyn St. Clair. (0-486-47360-0)

AUTHENTIC AMERICAN INDIAN BEADWORK AND HOW TO DO IT: WITH 50 CHARTS FOR BEAD WEAVING AND 21 FULL-SIZE PATTERNS FOR APPLIQUE, Pamela Stanley-Millner. (0-486-24739-2)

NORTH AMERICAN INDIAN BEADWORK PATTERNS, Pamela Stanley-Millner. (0-486-28835-8)

THE JOY OF HANDWEAVING, Osma Gallinger Tod. (0-486-23458-4)

KNOTS, SPLICES AND ROPE-WORK: AN ILLUSTRATED HANDBOOK, A. Hyatt Verrill. (0-486-44789-8)

HAND BOOKBINDING: A MANUAL OF INSTRUCTION, Aldren A. Watson. (0-486-29157-X)

See every Dover book in print at www.doverpublications.com